# IMAGES OF FIRE

*Into action with West Yorkshire
Fire & Rescue Service*

*Neil Wallington*

*1974 map of West Yorkshire showing fire stations.*

This book is dedicated to both the past and current uniformed and civilian personnel of West Yorkshire Fire & Rescue Service and its constituent Brigades prior to 1974, in recognition of their dedicated and selfless service to the community.

# FOREWORD

WEST YORKSHIRE IS the most built-up and largest urban area within the historic county boundaries of Yorkshire. West Yorkshire was formed as a metropolitan county in 1974, by the Local Government Act 1972, and corresponds roughly to the core of the historic West Riding of Yorkshire and the county boroughs of Bradford, Dewsbury, Halifax, Huddersfield, Leeds, and Wakefield.

The 1972 Act abolished previous existing local government structures, and created a two-tier system of counties and districts everywhere. Some of the new counties were designated metropolitan counties, containing metropolitan boroughs/districts instead. The allocation of functions differed between the metropolitan and the non-metropolitan areas, the so-called 'shire counties'. For example, education and social services were the responsibility of the shire counties, but in metropolitan areas was given to the districts.

The West Riding of Yorkshire was one of the three historic sub-divisions of Yorkshire. Its boundaries roughly corresponded to the present ceremonial counties of West Yorkshire, South Yorkshire and the Craven, Harrogate and Selby districts of North Yorkshire, along with smaller parts of Lancashire, Cumbria, Greater Manchester and, since 1996, the unitary East Riding of Yorkshire.

West Yorkshire Metropolitan County Council inherited the use of West Riding County Hall at Wakefield, opened in 1898, from the West Riding County Council in 1974. The county initially had a two-tier structure of local government with a strategic-level county council and five district councils providing most services. In 1986, throughout England the metropolitan county councils were abolished. The functions of the county council were devolved to the districts with joint-boards covering fire, police and public transport

and to other special joint arrangements. Organisations such as West Yorkshire Police Authority, the Fire Authority and West Yorkshire Passenger Transport Executive continue to operate on this basis.

West Yorkshire, which is landlocked, consists of five metropolitan districts (City of Bradford, Calderdale, Kirklees, City of Leeds and City of Wakefield) and shares borders with the counties of Derbyshire (to the south), Greater Manchester (to the south-west), Lancashire (to the north-west), North Yorkshire (to the north and east) and South Yorkshire (to the south-east). West Yorkshire has a population of 2.2 million.

West Yorkshire Fire & Rescue Service is the county-wide, statutory emergency fire and rescue service. It is administered by a joint authority of twenty-two ward councillors who are appointed annually from the five metropolitan districts of West Yorkshire, known as the Fire and Rescue Authority.

West Yorkshire covers an area of approximately 800 square miles (2,000 square kilometres), which includes remote moorland, rural villages and large towns and cities as well as Leeds Bradford International Airport. The fire and rescue service's headquarters are located at Oakroyd Hall, Bradford Road, Birkenshaw, between Bradford and Cleckheaton. West Yorkshire Fire & Rescue Service is funded by central government, Leeds City Council, City of Bradford Metropolitan District Council, Wakefield City Council, Calderdale Council and Kirklees Council.

West Yorkshire Fire & Rescue Service has developed and evolved in very many ways over the last forty years, both technologically and culturally, and now provides a range of public safety services and operational capabilities that are focused on reducing the risk of emergency incidence, whilst at the same time remaining prepared and ready to respond to people and businesses requiring its help. The Service is very proud of its fire prevention and protection performance having exceeded targets for reducing accidental and deliberate fires as well as the number of fire-related deaths and injuries in the home. The Service is run very efficiently and effectively, underpinned by its ambition of 'Making West Yorkshire Safer'. Modern day equipment and protective clothing bear little comparison to the rudimentary items in use forty years ago, as I'm sure the reader will notice from several of the images in this book. A range of operational response capabilities, including Urban Search and Rescue (collapsed buildings) and High Volume Pumps (flooding) are now provided for both local, regional and national response.

This book is dedicated to all the men and women who have helped provide and deliver a tremendous service to the public and business communities of West Yorkshire over the last forty years. I would also like to pay lasting tribute to Fireman Jeff Naylor who paid the ultimate sacrifice when he died in July 1983, over two months after suffering severe burns attempting to rescue children from a house fire at Keighley. He was posthumously awarded the Queen's Commendation for Bravery. The fire also claimed the lives of two children; however, three youngsters were saved.

It is a privilege and an honour to lead such a magnificent public service organisation. I hope the images that span the forty years of West Yorkshire Fire & Rescue Service do justice to the bravery and dedication of firefighters and also demonstrate the skill and vision of our photographers.

**Simon Pilling** QFSM MA MSc DMA GIFIREE
**Chief Fire Officer And Chief Executive,**
**West Yorkshire Fire & Rescue Service**

# INTRODUCTION

I HAVE ALWAYS felt that photographs of raging fire and smoke from a burning building are probably some of the most dramatic scenes that the camera can ever capture. Although fire is probably man's oldest friend, in an uncontrolled form it can be a fearsome enemy and examples of this have been recorded since the early days of photography.

Using early glass plate cameras, Victorians occasionally gave us black and white photographic examples of brass-helmeted firemen and their horse-drawn steam fire engines at work. However, the coming of colour film in the twentieth century brought a whole new graphic dimension to recording the drama and potential dangers of firefighting.

Few of today's British public fire brigades have an operational in-house photographic unit manned by a dedicated team that operates twenty-four hours a day. One of those that does is West Yorkshire Fire & Rescue Service. For four decades, a photographic team has recorded the work of firefighters in the area, including at serious accidents and a variety of other emergencies that go to make up the operational work of a modern Fire and Rescue Service.

A number of the major fires of the last forty years or so attended by the Brigade have involved some of the historic large mill complexes that abound across West Yorkshire. Nowadays, few of these operate as working mills. Some are unoccupied or part-derelict and are targets for arson attacks. Due to the combustible nature of these buildings, whose structures contain a considerable amount of timber, an outbreak of fire in an old mill often develops very rapidly into a major conflagration that can require all the skills, physical stamina and bravery of a hundred firefighters or more before control of the angry and fearsome flames is achieved.

Even during the days of monochrome film, and certainly since colour became widely used, the images of fire captured over the past forty years by West Yorkshire photographers have set new standards in modern photography, including national awards for excellence. Brigade photographers invariably have to work amongst some very difficult and challenging situations, often close to the action near to a fast-developing fire and its thick toxic smoke. And when major blazes occur during the dark hours as they frequently do, the photographic results can be even more spectacular as this book illustrates throughout its pages.

Since those early days of its inception, the thousands of images captured by the West Yorkshire Visual Services Photographic Team have provided evidence for fire investigation into the causes of fire and detailed forensic scene-of-fire support in conjunction with West Yorkshire Police and the Coroner's Office when fatalities, arson or other crime is suspected. The images also provide invaluable training material when firefighting operations are analysed on a regular basis. In more recent years, the Photographic Team have gone on to produce educational and training material including videos and other commercially available items concerning fire safety and prevention for use by industry, commerce and the community at large.

It was back in the 1970s when I was writing my first fire service books that my attention was drawn to the superb photographic work of the West Yorkshire Fire Service and its original photographer, Brian Saville. Subsequently, the extremely high quality of the West Yorkshire images regularly brought an added dimension to my various titles, as these photographs went far beyond that which an ordinary press photographer could ever secure, remote from the close action behind the police cordon at a fire or other emergency scene.

Consequently, when I began to plan a volume of images to reflect the round-the-clock work of a modern Fire & Rescue Service, it was to West Yorkshire that I came.

The British Fire Service is the nation's premier front-line emergency service, and at the scene of most major fires and emergency incidents, whilst the public are fast fleeing in the opposite direction to seek safety, fire crews will be heading towards the smoke and flames, the accident site, chemical spillage, gas explosion or whatever hazard might face them.

This book is primarily my personal tribute to the photographic skills so ably demonstrated over the years by Brian Saville, Andrew Hanson and Ken Wilkinson at West Yorkshire Fire & Rescue Service. However, I sincerely hope that these dramatic images of West Yorkshire firefighters at work also convey something of the selfless commitment of firefighters elsewhere across the nation's Fire and Rescue Services as they stand ready, both night and day in all weathers, to protect life and property from whatever dangerous challenges another fire or other emergency might throw at them.

Neil Wallington
**Bourne, Lincolnshire**
**March 2014**

# THE PUBLISHER

I AM VERY pleased and honoured to publish this title to coincide with the fortieth Anniversary of the founding of the modern West Yorkshire Fire & Rescue Service and the opening of the new Service Delivery Centre at Leeds.

The inspiration for this title came from a remarkable man, an heroic and dedicated firefighter and an extraordinary public servant. These three roles are the attributes of one man; the author Mr Neil Wallington, a time-served firefighter and former Chief Fire Officer.

Neil and I first met over twenty years ago when he travelled to Huddersfield in West Yorkshire and we worked together to redesign *The Journal of the Institution of Fire Engineers*. Since then, Neil, along with his continuing work with Fire and Rescue organisations throughout the world, has authored numerous successful fire and rescue titles, many of which I have had the privilege to publish. Nearly all of these are still in print and can be ordered directly from my company (see page 123 for details or visit our bookshop at www.firebookshop.co.uk).

Since we first met, I have been fortunate to see my one man business grow into a small group of companies, The Dunn & Mills Group, run by myself and Mr Charles Dunn my business partner, which now employs over eighty staff (many of these in the West Yorkshire region) engaged in publishing, printing and bookbinding. It is, therefore, with considerable pleasure that after twenty years Neil and I have been able to work together once again, but this time on a book dedicated to West Yorkshire which has been designed, printed and bound in the County.

I acknowledge the considerable trust vested in me by Chief Fire Officer Simon Pilling to accurately represent and showcase the extraordinary work of his brigade and his dedicated staff. Their

considerable input and wise counsel in conjunction with the author's experience and knowledge has been invaluable.

My publishing team working with the author and the Brigade have sought to showcase the exceptional and dramatic, award-winning photography of Brian Saville and his team. I think they have succeeded admirably in bringing to life the many major incidents and heroic work of the Brigade in the last forty years. I extend my personal thanks to Hazel Goodes, my Publishing Manager and Dawn Cockcroft, my designer for their excellent work.

Finally, to you the reader, thank you for buying this book. Your purchase has made a contribution to helping us to employ skilled staff in the printing and publishing sector in West Yorkshire and to promote the excellent work of the West Yorkshire Fire & Rescue Service.

**Jeremy Mills**
**Publisher**

**Huddersfield, West Yorkshire**
**March 2014**

# WEST YORKSHIRE AND ITS
# FIRE & RESCUE SERVICE:
# AN HISTORICAL PERSPECTIVE

WEST YORKSHIRE IS the most built-up and largest urban area within the historic county boundaries of Yorkshire. Whilst Leeds is the UK's second financial centre outside of London and is a vibrant, growing city, West Yorkshire also has areas of deprivation, while being surrounded by more affluent neighbourhoods, countryside and small villages, and is ethnically, culturally and geographically diverse.

## THE METROPOLITAN BOROUGHS

**Leeds** district embraces the county's largest city, and has a population of around 750,000, who are made up of 130 different nationalities, and covers an area of approximately 213 square miles. Leeds has a number of high risk sites, including two major hospitals, two large sports stadia and several large shopping outlets, and a number of large industrial sites. The area's main transport links are Leeds Bradford International Airport, Leeds Railway Station, the M1, M62 and M621 motorways and A1 trunk road. The Halifax/Huddersfield to Gildersome section of the M62 Trans-Pennine motorway is widely reported as one of the most congested sections of motorway in the country. Leeds is home to the successful East Leeds Young Firefighters scheme and the district includes a community safety department and arson task force.

**Bradford** district is in the north west of the county. It covers an area of approximately 140 square miles and has a population of more than 500,000. Bradford district is also an economically challenged area, containing a large range of socio-economic groups from the wealthy to the very deprived. These factors create a wide variety of risk profiles that West Yorkshire Fire & Rescue Service must monitor carefully through operational staff in conjunction with a dedicated community safety team, arson task force and fire safety department. Much of the effectiveness of the district's community safety strategy lies in the links with local authority partners.

**Calderdale** district covers an area of 140 square miles and has a population of around 200,100. It contains large areas of open countryside and moorland, as well as several deprived areas. The district has some 4,000 listed buildings and the largest town, Halifax, still retains one of the most complete Victorian landscapes in Britain. Calderdale district provides a water rescue capability where firefighters are specially trained to deal with flooding and rescuing people trapped in water emergencies that can follow heavy rain. In addition, there is a wildfire unit with specially trained personnel who can deal with large scale moorland or grass fires.

**Kirklees** is one of the largest metropolitan districts in England and Wales, with a population of 404,000 spread over an area of 157 square miles. The area is a contrast between remote, rural areas and town centres such as Huddersfield and Dewsbury. It includes a major motorway (the M62) and rail network, together with risks such as the five kilometre long Standedge tunnel under the Pennines, three major hospitals and seven sites that come under the Control of Major Accident Hazards (COMAH) legislation due to their storage and use of hazardous substances. Kirklees has a history of strong partnership work, which continues to go from strength to strength.

**Wakefield** district covers some 219 square miles and is home to 315,000 people in a diverse range of city, urban and rural communities. Since the demise of the coal mining industry, the district has become the base for a number of distribution and manufacturing companies.

West Yorkshire Fire & Rescue Service is a key partner on a number of groups in the district, with focus on arson reduction, youth inclusion (such as the Young Firefighters scheme, which first started in Wakefield), fire safety enforcement, and road traffic collision reduction.

THE DEVELOPMENT OF WEST YORKSHIRE'S FIRE SERVICE

Historically, it was the industrial revolution which changed West Yorkshire from a group of small rural towns into the powerhouses of industry, leading to the growth of the woollen districts of Bradford, Huddersfield and Halifax and its associated industries of engineering and chemical production situated in the steep river valleys to the west of the county.

Leeds became Yorkshire's largest city with commerce and heavy industry, and Wakefield with the coal mining industry, glass production and chemicals. All these industries helped develop the prosperity of the region. As Yorkshire's prosperity grew, so did the lavish development of civic buildings with well-appointed structures being laid out by the city fathers. To protect this massive growth, civic responsibility called for commissioners of lighting and watching, and watch committees developed in the early 1800s. However, by the latter half of the nineteenth century, the six largest towns were 'incorporated' and the corporations developed fire brigades on a professional footing, setting the early foundations of today's modern Fire & Rescue Service.

Before the Second World War, most of the sixty or so towns within the region had created their own fire brigades or relied on their bigger neighbours to provide fire cover. The history of Leeds City Fire Brigade proudly goes back to the early 1800s, whereas others like Colne Valley were created prior to the onset of war, having relied upon private brigades belonging to the massive mills in the urban districts.

From August 1941, the various West Yorkshire brigades became part of the National Fire Service to provide fire cover across the region until the end of Second World War. In 1948, the National Fire Service was disbanded by the government and responsibility for fire service was returned to local authorities. These seven individual and unique brigades each with a proud history were the West Riding County Fire Service, Bradford City Fire Brigade, Leeds City Fire Brigade, Wakefield City Fire Brigade, Dewsbury County Borough Fire Brigade, Halifax County Borough Fire Brigade and Huddersfield County Borough Fire Brigade. Camaraderie, innovation and a pioneering spirit saw them develop into highly efficient brigades led by extremely well known and respected Chief Fire Officers.

SOME EARLY FIRE SERVICE HISTORICAL PERSONALITIES

Chief Henry Baker was known locally as the 'Fire King' and he equipped Leeds with the first 65-foot, wooden free-standing ladder from Magirus of Germany in the 1880s. It was a first in the region. Chief Baker entertained a large contingent of the Paris Fire Brigade in 1891 who presented him with the Médaille d'Honneur. In 1892 he led the firefighting effort at one of the biggest blazes ever to occur in Leeds when a huge store under the main railway station called the 'Dark Arches' packed with drums of flammable tallow and other stock ignited and burned for four days. It required the attendance of fire

**1903**

*Half Moon Street, Huddersfield. A 50ft wheeled escape ladder is in use. Image courtesy of Chris Smith.*

**1914**

*A horse drawn Merryweather steam pump at work in West Yorkshire with a motor pump in the far background. Image courtesy of Chris Smith.*

brigades from as far away as Bradford, York and Derby to extinguish the huge conflagration, but sadly not before it had claimed the life of Fireman James Potter Schofield. The fire loss was conservatively put at £20 million at today's prices.

Chief James Scott of Bradford travelled throughout Europe lecturing on fire safety and became President of the Professional Fire Officers Society. In 1908 Bradford was one of the first brigades outside of London to introduce the concept of a motorised fire engine. Built by Dennis Brothers of Guildford in Surrey and christened the 'Freeman', such was its advantage seen over horse power, that by 1914 Bradford had four such motor tenders and all the old machinery including the horses were sold off.

In those early days, a scarcity of motorised transport was such that a driver had to be employed and he and the Chief Fire Officer drove the lumbering beast all the way from Surrey to Bradford on solid tyres! Brigades came from far and wide to see the new wonder fire engine and soon were buying their own. In 1902 Bradford also had one of the foremost designs in new fire stations, with dignitaries coming from all over the world and the most prestigious brigades in the country to examine and copy the design.

During the Victorian and Edwardian period most of the firemen served their city or town for up to forty years and consequently saw many fires, large and small. Many were too numerous to mention, but the 1916 Low Moor munitions works explosion in Bradford stands out as one of the most devastating. This explosion killed six of Bradford's eighteen firemen and rendered the rest 'hors de combat' after one magazine caught fire, leading to a cascading explosion that was heard some 100 miles away. These men are honoured with two others of the Bradford Brigade on a 30-foot high statue of a firefighter in the grounds of West Yorkshire Fire & Rescue Service Headquarters at Birkenshaw. Other monuments and plaques also exist to honour the thirty-one firefighters who have lost their lives as a result of attending other incidents in the county.

**1900**

*Huddersfield Fire Station with the full complement of firemen and their machines on parade. Image courtesy of Chris Smith.*

**1910**

*This Dennis was one of Leeds Fire Brigade's first motor pumps and is carrying a 50ft wheeled escape ladder. Image courtesy of Chris Smith.*

**1912**

*Huddersfield Fire Station. Horses Manxman (left) and Tom pose for the camera with Sergeant Thompson (left). These horses were sold during the same year with the arrival of the first motorised pumps. In the background are some of the horse-drawn ladders. Image courtesy of Ray Banyard.*

To improve themselves and keep abreast of modern firefighting techniques, fire brigades grouped together to form the West Yorkshire Fire Brigades Friendly Society, led at one time by Sir Charles Firth, a local large mill owner and friend of the Prince of Wales. The 'gentlemen firemen' spread knowledge and good practice throughout the society and were aptly described by the Society's motto 'Bear ye one another's burdens'.

## WEST YORKSHIRE AND THE RISK OF MILL FIRES

Over one and a half centuries, the West Riding area had become world-renowned for fine cloth made in its textile mills. However, an adverse safety factor of these mills as they grew progressively older was that their wooden floors become oil-soaked from the task of taking wool through the manufacturing process. As can be seen in this sequence of dramatic images, a small fire can quickly build up and spread rapidly to the point of flashover and total involvement in flames, often within minutes of the initial outbreak.

Over the years, the West Yorkshire region has suffered many serious mill fires, some fatal. In 1818 at Atkinson's Mill in Huddersfield, eighteen children perished after being locked in a building overnight. A serious fire at Brookes in Huddersfield in 1941 led to mandatory improvements in means of escape requirements from large buildings after forty-nine people perished when the single existing stairway was consumed by flames. And the 1956 fire at Eastwood's Mill in Keighley led to amendments to the Factories Act after eight employees lost their lives due to a lack of fire safety measures following the careless use of a blow lamp.

Consequently, bringing firefighting and rescue resources to bear as quickly and as safely as possible to protect life and stop and control the fire by aggressive firefighting tactics has become part of the proud history inherited by West Yorkshire Fire & Rescue Service and its personnel.

*These images illustrate just how rapidly a small fire in a mill can turn into a raging inferno engulfing all floors of Commercial Mills, Slaithwaite, Huddersfield in 1969.*

## THE SECOND WORLD WAR AND AFTER

From August 1941, the various brigades of the West Yorkshire became part of the National Fire Service in order to provide fire cover across the region until the end of Second World War. In 1948, the National Fire Service was disbanded by the government and responsibility for the fire service was returned to local authorities.

The perfection of skills required to be a firefighter led to the opening of a new Training Centre at the West Riding Headquarters at Birkenshaw in 1961 by Chief Fire Officer Harry Judge, and such was his vision that he went on as its first Commandant thirteen years later to found the government-funded Fire Service Technical College at Moreton-in-Marsh in Gloucestershire, later renamed as the world-renowned Fire Service College.

It is this deep-rooted historical drive for excellence which has undoubtedly been passed down to today's firefighters and has engendered the highly respected professionals of the service through the ages.

*Chief Fire Officer Harry Judge.*

## THE 1974 LOCAL GOVERNMENT REORGANISATION

The local government reorganisation of 1974 changed the three ancient Ridings of Yorkshire, and created a large metropolitan area out of the old West Riding. Prior to this reorganisation, the region was huge, stretching from the Cumbrian border in the north to Derbyshire in the south, west to Lancashire and east to the coast and the East Riding.

On 1st April 1974, all seven separate brigades in the region were amalgamated to form the new West Yorkshire Fire Service. From the seven separate post-1948 fire brigades, Chief Fire Officer Kevin Horan of the West Riding was appointed Chief of the new West Yorkshire Fire Service, whilst the six other Chief Fire Officers – Jack Garside (Bradford), Fred Scott (Leeds), John Slack (Wakefield), Michael Dempsey (Dewsbury), John J. Hunsworth (Halifax) and Dennis Baker (Huddersfield) – all took senior command roles in the new organisation.

*Chief Fire Officer Kevin Horan.*

## THE ROUTE TO THE BRIGADE'S MODERN TITLE

On the abolition of West Yorkshire County Council in 1986, control of West Yorkshire Fire Service passed to the West Yorkshire Fire and Civil Defence Authority. In 2004, this body in turn was replaced by the creation of the West Yorkshire Fire & Rescue Authority following the enactment of the Fire & Rescue Services Act 2004. The Brigade's

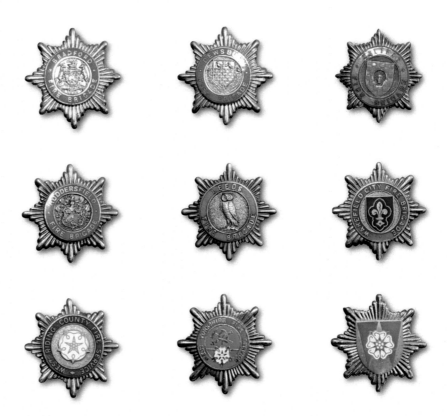

*The badges of the seven constituent fire brigades making up the enlarged 1974 West Yorkshire Fire Service.*

title then officially became West Yorkshire Fire & Rescue Service to reflect the new statutory responsibility given to fire brigades in addition to their historic firefighting duties.

Tragically, one of the last major emergency incidents to occur before the new West Yorkshire Fire Service assumed the mantle of firefighting and rescue response to incidents across the region was the M62 motorway coach bombing during the night of 4th February 1974. The coach was carrying British Army and Royal Air Force personnel en route on leave to their families and was proceeding along the M62. As the coach passed the Hartshead Moor service area, a large explosion occurred on board, where most of the servicemen were sleeping at the time. The blast, which could be heard several miles away, reduced the coach to a tangle of twisted metal, killing eleven persons outright and wounding over fifty others, one of whom died four days later.

## WEST YORKSHIRE'S MODERN FIRE & RESCUE SERVICE

The modern-day West Yorkshire Fire & Rescue Service has its Headquarters and Training School at Oakroyd Hall, Birkenshaw. The Brigade has approximately 1,220 wholetime firefighters, 170 retained (volunteer) firefighters, forty-seven firefighters manning the 999 control centre, and 260 specialist and support staff. There are

forty-six fire stations across West Yorkshire with a total of fifty-four pumping appliances, five aerial appliances, and numerous other specialist vehicles including water & line rescue and an urban search and rescue capability.

More detail regarding the structure of the Brigade and how it operates can be found in the Appendices to be found in the back pages of this book.

**Chief Fire Officers (Clockwise)**

*Fred Scott, Jack Garside, Dennis Baker, John Slack, John J. Hunsworth and Michael Dempsey.*

# IMAGES OF OPERATIONAL EMERGENCY INCIDENTS 1974–2014

ALL THE FOLLOWING images are taken from the Brigade's extensive photographic library, representing the operational front line work of the West Yorkshire Fire & Rescue Service photographic team over a period of forty years.

Unless otherwise shown, all photographs in this book are the copyright of West Yorkshire Fire & Rescue Service.

**1974      M62 Coach Bombing**

*Although West Yorkshire FRS did not come into being until April 1974, units of the old West Riding Fire Service did attend this major incident on the M62 motorway on 4th February when twelve members of the Armed Forces and several civilians were killed when a bomb, believed to have been planted by the IRA, exploded in the boot of the coach they were travelling in.*

**1975      Kirkgate Market, Leeds**

*One of the biggest fire disasters in Leeds was this huge blaze that, despite the valiant efforts of firefighters, all but destroyed Kirkgate Market, Europe's largest covered market. The cause was believed to be an overturned paraffin lamp and, fortunately, all 150 stallholders and many shoppers escaped as the flames took hold.*

**1975     Cullingworth Mills, Bradford**

*Firefighting in West Yorkshire has frequently involved the many historic mills going back to Victorian times. These multi-storey timber-floored premises were very vulnerable to rapid fire spread. This is the scene at Cullingworth Mills, Bradford, when this serious fire has been brought largely under control, although parts of the upper floors have fallen in. Senior officers of the Brigade are conferring with the mill occupiers.*

**1976     Bruntcliffe Mills, Morley (Overleaf)**

*A graphic view of another serious mill fire, where despite the physical efforts of many firefighters working in arduous and dangerous conditions, part of the roof of the mill has collapsed. This firefighter is silhouetted against the flames at the head of a 100ft turntable ladder.*

**1979     Debenhams, Manningham**

*West Yorkshire fire crews gain some respite from the considerable radiated heat behind cooling water jets during firefighting operations.*

**1980      Nostell Priory, Wakefield**

*This view of a serious fire at this historic West Yorkshire house, taken after the blaze had come under control, clearly illustrates the successful efforts of firefighters in containing the fire to part of the ground and first floor area. Outbreaks of fire in old country houses always pose a problem to fire crews as the construction of these buildings often present a challenge in restricting potential fire spread.*

**1980      Nostell Priory, Wakefield**

*The major fire at Nostell Priory threatened not only the structure and fabric of the historic house, but very many irreplaceable items of furniture and works of art. This view of a dining room shows where the fire has been stopped at the door on the far left, showing very little damage to the room and its contents.*

**1980     Light Aircraft Crash, Leeds Bradford Airport**

*West Yorkshire firefighters were quickly on the wintery scene with a foam attack in support of the airport fire service when this twin engine light aircraft skidded on landing and crashed through a perimeter fence in the snowy conditions. Fortunately there was no fire or serious injury.*

**1981    Bus Crash, Hellfire Corner, Wyke, Bradford**

*Emergency services were soon in attendance at the scene of this double-decker bus that had left the road and overturned. The bus suffered substantial bodywork damage and the driver and a number of passengers received serious injuries.*

**1982    Universal Freight, Woodkirk**

*This warehouse fire quickly also became a full scale chemical incident due to the storage of herbicides, octylphenol and other toxic substances in drums and plastic bottles causing major pollution alert to the public. This image shows the source of the fire and its damage to stored chemicals.*

**1983    Wyke Manor School, Bradford**

*During the early stages of firefighting operations, a 75ft hydraulic platform is positioned to get to work with a water jet to restrict the fire spread in the school roof.*

**1983      Denholme Fibres, Bradford**

*A view of this mill fire, about an hour after the first 999 call, when all firefighters had been withdrawn from inside the building due to the dangerous severity of the fire conditions. Fifteen pumps were called to deal with this outbreak.*

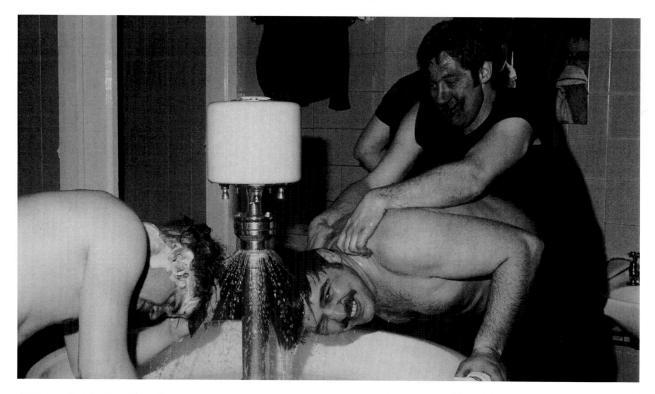

**1983      Cleaning Up, Old Nelson Street Fire Station, Bradford**

*Following their return from a working fire call, the camera catches this somewhat grubby West Yorkshire duty watch as it carries out basic ablutions, accompanied by some friendly horseplay. This photograph, taken by West Yorkshire Fire & Rescue Service photographer Brian Saville, was one of several that won national awards for their excellence.*

**1984     Arnold Laver, Bradford**

*This former huge mill building was trading as a cash-and-carry warehouse when the Brigade was called to a small fire on the upper floor. This scene is what actually faced the first West Yorkshire fire crews arriving at the site. Even as they got to work, the fire spread with frightening intensity typical of an old mill fire and ultimately developed into a twenty pump incident. For another view of this fire, see page 21.*

**1984        Summit Rail Tunnel**

*One of the more spectacular and physically challenging fires tackled by West Yorkshire firefighters, in conjunction with Lancashire fire crews, was that in the Summit rail tunnel through the Pennines. The fire originated when a fuel train was derailed inside the tunnel, igniting one of the rail tankers. The fire spread to other tankers and burned for several days making access into the tunnel extremely difficult. The left hand view shows the fire and smoke pouring forth from the tunnel ventilation shafts high up in the Pennines some hours after the derailment. The fearsome flame column emerging high above the hill roared for many hours across the valley as the fire in the tunnel below consumed thousands of gallons of fuel.*

*Once the fire was finally extinguished using copious supplies of foam, the incident became one of damping down, making safe and clearing up the vast amount of equipment used during the operation.*

**1986    Bowling Back Lane, Bradford**

*This unusual image, caught by Brigade photographer Brian Saville, shows the flames of this warehouse fire reflected upon the windscreen of one of West Yorkshire's new Dennis pumps.*

**1986    Fatal House Fire, Brighouse**

*This dramatic photograph encapsulates a firefighter's primary task – that of rescue. These two crew members have just emerged from a search of a very hot and smoke-filled bedroom for missing persons in this early morning house fire. Sadly they have only been able to locate a lifeless body. Having removed their breathing apparatus facemasks, the steam rising from their uniforms and their grim facial expressions say it all.*

**1985     Bradford City Football Club, Valley Parade**

*Using his helmet to protect his face from the heat, a policeman runs across the pitch as flames sweep through the stands at Bradford City football club, after fire started in a pile of rubbish under seating. Charred discarded clothing and policemen's helmets, lost in the rescue efforts, lie around the field. The fire developed extremely rapidly in the wooden stand, engulfing the entire structure within minutes. Fifty-six spectators died in the inferno and many victims were found piled up against the locked exit barriers behind the stand. Many survivors suffered serious burns. The subsequent inquiry led to a new Fire Safety Act that required more stringent fire safety measures in sports stadiums and recreational venues (Telegraph & Argus).*

**1986      Moderna Mills, Mytholmroyd**

*The sheer scale of some old disused mill fires is evident in this photograph where the combustible nature of the structure has given firefighters little chance to save the building. Note the two 100ft turntable ladders working as water towers at each end of the fire front.*

**1987      Wall Collapse, Sackville Road, Bradford**

*Several hundred tons of coal cascaded into the street when this wall suddenly collapsed. Fire crews are digging frantically to ensure that no casualties are buried beneath the coal.*

**1987     House Fire, Allerton, Bradford**

*A Leading Fireman tenderly carries a young child to a waiting ambulance following his snatch rescue from a smoke filled house. A second child was successfully rescued from this house fire and is here being taken to the waiting ambulance.*

**1987     House Fire, Allerton, Bradford**

*This much happier related photograph, taken some weeks after the fire, shows the two affected children following their discharge from hospital and making a full recovery. The children's father is on the left, whilst on the right is West Yorkshire Fire & Rescue Service photographer Brian Saville, who took the original photograph of their rescue. This incident led to a decision by Bradford Council to fit smoke detection in all council flats.*

**1987      Horse Rescue, Bradford**

*Despite protecting a primarily highly urban area, West Yorkshire fire crews do occasionally have some unusual non-fire emergencies to deal with, including the rescue of animals. This horse has collapsed in a field and the fire crew is working to support the animal prior to the arrival of a vet. Fortunately the horse survived.*

**1988      Pennine Fibres, Denholme**

*Any major outbreak of fire demands significant and reliable supplies of firefighting water, and part of a firefighter's skill and science is to maximise every available water source near to the incident. This photograph taken during this serious mill fire shows one of a number of light portable pumps drawing water from a pond adjacent to the fire.*

**1988      K & N Fashions, Roundhay Road, Leeds**

*Occasionally when the first fire crews arrive at the scene only a few minutes after a 999 call, the fire situation can already be well developed as in the case of this clothing warehouse. The first firefighting jets are being brought to bear as a 100ft turntable ladder in the background also gets to work. Breathing apparatus crews will shortly begin a search of the smoke filled building, in which a fatal casualty was located.*

**1989     BA Crew, Farnley School, Leeds**

*Firefighting is physically demanding, uncomfortable and often dangerous. In this image this member of a West Yorkshire breathing apparatus team is descending into the basement to carry out some damping down after the main fire has been mostly extinguished. In a situation such as this, the value of a firefighter's regular training routines and team work are critical.*

**1989      A1 near the M62 Intersection**

*This fire started within the articulated lorry's trailer contents and by the time West Yorkshire Fire & Rescue Service crews managed to reach the scene through the gridlocked traffic, the flames had spread to engulf the tractor unit. When he first noticed the fire in the trailer, the lorry driver pulled off onto the hard shoulder where the radiated heat quickly ignited the nearby hedgerows and trees, giving the firefighting teams plenty to contend with using a foam and water fog attack. The camera captures the final minutes before the blaze comes under control.*

**1989      Acid spillage, Lock Lane, Castleford (Right)**

*During the 1980s there was a steady growth of non-fire emergencies for fire brigades to deal with. West Yorkshire crews were increasingly being called out to deal with a range of these incidents such as this spillage of acid from drums which have fallen from a lorry. Fire crews rigged in full chemical protection suits and breathing apparatus are using absorbent material to mop up the spillage. This protracted operation will be followed by the decontamination of all the personnel concerned.*

**1989      Rescue of Cow, Odsal, Bradford**

*This series of photographs records the remarkable rescue of a cow which became trapped when it fell into a hole. The successful rescue of the animal was a careful and protracted operation involving digging, ropes, slings, plenty of muscle power and much patience of the fire crew involved. The final image shows the extremely grimy yet happy faces of the West Yorkshire firefighters who successfully carried out this unusual rescue.*

**1990    Overturned Chemical Tanker, Oulton, Leeds**

*Another view of a specialist non-fire emergency operation involving a crew dressed in chemical protection suits and breathing apparatus at the scene of a chemical tanker that has overturned at a roundabout. In event of fire, the crew are ready with a water spray to the underside of the tanker whilst other firefighters, who are out of view, are preventing the spillage from entering the drains.*

**1990    Beta Lighting, Bradford**

*As the atmosphere clears once this fire has been extinguished, this crew in breathing apparatus (BA) view some of the hazards that they have navigated during the thick smoke of the earlier firefighting operation. Regular BA training always puts an emphasis on the safety of BA wearers in smoke-filled buildings where nil visibility is often the norm.*

**1990    LPG Explosion and Fire, Huddersfield**

*When gas cylinders are involved in a fire situation they always add another dangerous dimension for firefighters. In the aftermath of this ten pump fire, West Yorkshire Fire and Rescue investigators suspected that this liquid petroleum gas (LPG) cylinder was a possible cause of the outbreak when flammable vapour leaked from the cylinder.*

**1990     Watmoughs Printers, Idle, Bradford**

*Modern man-made materials, including plastics, when involved in fire have greatly increased the toxicity of smoke. As a consequence, firefighters increasingly resort to wearing breathing apparatus (BA) for their respiratory protection. Firefighters regularly train in BA to maximise safety and practise search procedures for when working in thick smoke. Here, this BA crew is going through the safety log-in procedure at a control point before entering the smoked-logged print works as part of the firefighting operation.*

**1990     Gas Explosion, Franklin Street, Halifax (Overleaf)**

*Explosions involving leaking gas can cause extensive damage to a structure as is shown in this view of a terraced property where both floors and the frontage have been completely blown out into the street. Fire crews are checking for casualties and using a hydraulic platform to make parts of the roof safe.*

**1990     Bakers Haulage, Bradford (Pages 50-51)**

*One of the largest fires dealt with by West Yorkshire Fire & Rescue Service in its recent history was this twenty-five pump fire involving a haulage company's warehouse complex. Major fires during the dark hours have a drama all of their own as can be seen from this view of firefighters getting additional lines of hose to work against a background of a fast-spreading fire situation. The radiated heat being given off is almost palpable.*

**1991     Cheapside, Bradford**

*The day after the serious fire at Cheapside, Bradford, Brian Saville, the Head of West Yorkshire's Visual Aid Department is himself caught on camera as he moves around the fire damaged building taking photographs. Some damage was caused to Bradford Exchange railway platforms by the falling debris from the fire the night before.*

**1991     North Street, Bradford**

*Another dramatic example of rapid fire spread in a West Yorkshire old mill building taken only minutes after the first of many 999 calls and the arrival of the first firefighting crews. In this view, an 85ft hydraulic platform is being got to work, as the rampant flames remorselessly spread the fire into the upper floors.*

**1991     Cheapside, Bradford (Left)**

*When fire spreads very rapidly within a large building complex, at some stage fire commanders at the scene can be faced with a decision to withdraw firefighters from inside the building when their safety might be compromised. From that point on, the firefighting strategy becomes one to surround the burning building with multiple water jets to protect adjacent premises. This image shows an external water curtain as crews have been withdrawn from this large warehouse blaze and the emphasis is now to maintain sufficient firefighting water supplies.*

**1991    North Street, Bradford**

*This image was taken about thirty minutes later, showing the building well surrounded by firefighting jets which are in turn protecting the adjacent unaffected buildings from fire spread and radiated heat. However, there is still plenty of hard physical work ahead and the crews will be on the scene well into the night hours.*

**1991    Watmoughs Printers, Idle**

*Working safely at heights is all part of a firefighter's training and culture. With the fire under control, these two firefighters are working off a 45ft ladder in order to open windows, ventilate and clear the smoke from the upper floors. Note both firefighters have taken a safety 'leg lock' on the ladder.*

**1991    Tankards Mill, Dewsbury (Right)**

*Water is still the primary extinguishing agent at large building fires. The crew in the cage of this 85ft hydraulic platform gets an effective aerial water jet to work on yet another mill fire. In fire service parlance this is known as 'getting the wet stuff on the hot stuff'. The estimated loss of this particular fire was put at £2.5 million.*

**1991     M62 Road Traffic Collision, Wakefield (Left)**

*From around the late 1960s, the fire service was being called more frequently to the scenes of road traffic collisions where driver and passengers were trapped. These emergencies were further complicated by the opening of more motorways and their consequent high speed accidents. This image shows the rescue operation of a lorry driver who is trapped in his cab following a winter-time collision. The fire service was instrumental in the introduction of new high powered cutting and lifting equipment for incidents such as this.*

**1992     Hickson & Welch, Wheldon Road, Castleford**

*This major incident required the attendance of twenty-two fire engines and over 100 firefighters when an explosion and fire caused nine fatalities and widespread devastation across this industrial chemical plant site. During a routine cleaning operation a distillation tank of nitrotoluene ignited, causing a fireball that went through the site's control room and killed two employees instantly. The fireball then entered a four storey office block, causing further fatalities. 800 people were employed on the site and 200 of these were injured. When West Yorkshire Fire & Rescue Service crews arrived they were faced with the challenge of controlling a number of separate fires.*

**1992    Allied Colloids, Bradford (Left and above)**

*The explosion and fire at Allied Colloids chemical plant initiated one of the largest mobilisations in the Brigade's history, resulting in serious pollution up to 30km away. The first fire crews on the scene were called to smoke issuing from a warehouse in the complex and fire broke out after two explosions which spread fire to a large quantity of drums of liquids, powders and plastics. The flames rapidly became very intense with liquid products flowing out of the warehouse; a flashover turned the running liquid into a burning stream which eventually spread the fire into stored drums in remote parts of the site. The officer-in-charge requested further assistance and as the fire grew in proportions to involve 2,800 square metres of stored plastics and drums of various products, a total of twenty-five pumps and two turntable ladders were soon in attendance. Firefighters wearing breathing apparatus were able to save a main warehouse from serious damage despite drums falling through its roof following the explosions. The National Rivers Authority and the local water authority were informed of the consequences of the fire and police advised local residents to stay inside their houses and shut doors and windows due to the toxicity of the dense smoke plume. Sadly, five people lost their lives as a result of the fire and 150 were injured, including thirty-nine West Yorkshire firefighters.*

**1993     Bolton Brow, Sowerby Bridge, Halifax (Right and above)**

*When an eight-wheeled runaway lorry with defective brakes crashed into a BT van and then ploughed into a sub-post office a number of persons were trapped in the wreckage. Working with a medical team, West Yorkshire fire crews were faced with a very difficult and protracted operation and using a range of powerful rescue tools also had to support the weakened building shop front. This accident accounted for six fatalities, including both drivers and a mother and her two-year-old child.*

**1994      Spring Mill Street, Bradford**

*This unoccupied large mill was the subject of an arson attack where it was suspected that several fires were lit. This dramatic image was captured only minutes after the first West Yorkshire fire engines arrived and shows firefighting jets working from the pump on the left and in the far right distance an aerial ladder platform at work. Firefighters were challenged in saving the building by the rapidity of fire spread due to the flammability of the timber structure of the mill.*

**1994      Shop Collapse, Horsforth, Leeds**

*Explosions following a gas leak can be devastating as can be seen in this image of a collapsed shop. Having located a buried person, fire crews and a medical team are treating the casualty prior to removal to hospital.*

**1995     Withins Moor, Halifax**

*During the warmer months of the year, the incidence of grass and heathland fires increases significantly, and protracted spells of hot weather can result in major commitments by firefighters to deal with outbreaks that can cover a wide geographical area. Here, the camera captures crews as they set-to with beaters to tackle yet another summertime incident.*

**1995     Chemical Decontamination Exercise**

*The increasing incidence of hazardous materials involved in a fire situation or a leakage situation requires firefighters to wear various levels of protection according to the risk posed by the particular hazard of the substance involved. Here, during an exercise a firefighter undergoes full decontamination using equipment that has become a fire service standard on front line fire engines.*

1995 — Netto supermarket, Keighley

*A dramatic view of a BA crew crouching against the radiated heat, as they are about to get a powerful covering water jet to work at one end of a building that is already heavily involved in fire.*

1995     Crofton High School, Wakefield

*Fifteen West Yorkshire pumps were needed to control this major night-time blaze in the school and this image was taken when fireground commanders had withdrawn all crews from inside the building due to the rapidly spreading fire. All crews present anticipated the dawn and the considerable clearing-up operation that would inevitably follow. The financial cost of this and similar school fires can be*

**1995     Bus Depot, Torre Road, Leeds**

*An arson attack on the main Leeds bus garage caused major damage to a number of the city's buses. Here, having brought the fire under control, firefighters are damping down the smouldering remains of the severely damaged vehicles.*

**1995     Hemsworth Water Park, Kinsley**

*This was a particularly tragic non-fire emergency during a very icy spell of cold weather. A dog had fallen through the ice of a frozen lake and Michael Mee, an off-duty South Yorkshire firefighter who happened to be in the park, immediately went to the rescue, along with another passer-by and an eleven-year-old girl. All three fell through the ice and died. Here, West Yorkshire firefighters, some in protective suits, are searching for the casualties.*

**1997     George Street, Milnsbridge, Huddersfield   (Right)**

*This view shows an equally important part of firefighting operations, compared to the 'sharp end' closer to the fire. This outbreak developed into a fifteen pump attendance and this image illustrates two pumping appliances and their crews supplying critical firefighting water to colleagues at the fire front. Much physical work will already have taken place to lay out the hose lines, not to mention the hard graft of making up all equipment when the incident has finally come under control, some hours later.*

**1998      Almondbury Junior School, Huddersfield**

*Arson in schools is a particular national problem for fire services and West Yorkshire is no exception to this, having suffered a number of such arson attacks. Many of these incidents have developed into major conflagrations. This view taken when this fire was fully extinguished shows the total damage to a cloakroom area of the school, putting the entire establishment out of action for a considerable time.*

**1998      Trench Rescue, Yeadon**

*The camera captures the moment when an eighteen-year-old construction worker was finally rescued after being entombed down a 20ft deep trench for twelve hours when tons of wet soil suddenly collapsed and pinned him down under a boulder. West Yorkshire fire crews were assisted in this protracted and difficult extrication by a team from Mines Rescue. Hospital doctors were unable to save one of the casualty's legs, but he did survive to tell the tale of his long ordeal.*

**1998    Fuel Tanker, Oulton, Woodlesford, Leeds**

*Firefighting operations always rely on teamwork based upon regular continuation training, for at real-life incidents rapid decisions and actions need to be taken when life and property is at immediate risk. This image was taken after this West Yorkshire crew were called to an overturned articulated fuel tanker carrying 6,000 gallons of petrol and fuel oil. After a concentrated foam attack pressed home in the face of some danger, Leading firefighter Peter Buckland (centre) and his mostly young crew face the camera and emphasise the 'Father and Sons' teamwork that has taken place.*

**1998    Albert Mills, Dewsbury**

*Mill fires can be even more spectacular, dangerous and difficult to tackle at night.*

**1999    Fuel Tanker, M62**

*Two dramatic images of an intense fire in a loaded petrol tanker – the fire was probably caused by an over-heated brake spreading into the structure of the tanker and igniting its flammable contents. The second image shows a firefighting team attacking the fire, progressively working towards extinguishing the blaze with a foam jet.*

**1999    Vulcanite, High Street Castleford, Wakefield**

*A typical view of West Yorkshire fire engines at work at a serious fire. The two pumps on the left are each providing hose lines to crews working close to the seat of the fire, whilst the aerial ladder platform is well positioned to deliver a powerful jet from above the fire scene. This image stresses the importance of continuity training with its emphasis on the effective tactical deployment of fire engines on the fireground.*

**1999     Tong Garden Centre, Bradford (Left and above)**

*When the first crews were called to Yorkshire's biggest garden centre the fire had already taken a strong hold and was spreading rapidly across the complex. Fifteen pumps and 100 firefighters were quickly deployed and although they prevented the fire spreading into adjoining premises, the 60,000 square feet premises and its contents were severely damaged with an estimated loss of £2.7 million.*

**1999    Meadow Road, Greengates, Bradford**

*When West Yorkshire fire crews were called to this textile factory they found a male employee trapped in a bailing machine. The seriously injured casualty was in a very difficult position in a confined space and access to the machine was problematic. Using heavy powerful hydraulic rescue equipment and assisted by medical and paramedical teams the man was released after two hours' painstaking work and taken to hospital for specialist treatment.*

**1999    Whingate, Armley, Leeds (Right)**

*When fire broke out on the lower floor of this metal fabrication workshop, two employees tragically died when they were unable to escape down the stairs to safety as that route was cut off due to thick smoke and flames. It is thought that the fire originated in the storage of flammable paints and gas cylinders stored at the bottom of the stairs. Here, firefighters carefully lower one of the fatalities to ground floor level against the backdrop of the smoked blackened building.*

2000    Carlton Bolling College, Bradford

*Another major incident which illustrated the potential destruction caused by deliberately-lit fires was that which occurred at this college. Through their valiant efforts, West Yorkshire firefighters were able to save parts of the structure but the financial cost and educational disruption was huge.*

**2000     Flooding, Keighley**

*With the increasing incidence of wild weather, including flooding, the Brigade introduced new specialist vehicles and equipment to deal with the ensuing emergencies. Here an eight wheel all-terrain vehicle is shown at work during serious flooding following prolonged heavy rainfall that caused the River Aire to burst its banks.*

**2000     Dewsbury Dyeing Co (Left and above)**

*Many firefighting operations increasingly require the wearing of breathing apparatus (BA) to protect crews from the effects of toxic smoke. Since the 1950s the safety of BA wearers has been paramount and seen a progressive development of safety control procedures whenever BA is worn at an incident. Here, a BA control officer outside the fire monitors the personal tallies of the BA wearers at work inside the building, alert to when these crews should emerge into fresh air when their air supplies are low. An emergency crew in BA is standing by.*

*With firefighting still in progress, the above image captures two fire commanders in discussion over progress of operations at an advanced stage of the incident. The officer in a white helmet on the right is now the Chief Fire Officer and Chief Executive of West Yorkshire Fire & Rescue Service, Simon Pilling.*

**2000        Brigshaw High School, Allerton Bywater, Leeds (Left)**

*A BA crew with a hose line prepare to make an entry into the smoke-filled main corridor of the school with the severe night-time fire already developing further into the back of the complex. Twenty pumps and 100 firefighters were called to the scene. Following forensic investigation by West Yorkshire Fire & Rescue Service and the police, a sixteen-year-old boy was charged with arson following theft from the school and sentenced to detention for four years. The fire destroyed thirty classrooms, science laboratories, offices and dining areas. Irreplaceable GCSE and 'A' Level course work was also lost. The estimated financial fire loss was put at £7 million.*

**2000        Gas Explosion, East Street, Batley**

*Some idea of the explosive damage caused by leaking gas is demonstrated by this aerial view, taken some time after the blast that virtually demolished an end-of-terrace house and damaged surrounding properties. Protective hose lines have been laid out, and search and rescue crews have done their work. Sadly, two people lost their lives.*

**2001        Pallet Yard, Horbury, Wakefield**

*Despite the rapid attendance of West Yorkshire firefighters, a small fire in a yard quickly spread to hundreds of stacked wooden pallets. The radiant heat generated was immense and fire crews worked against walls of flames as they worked to surround the fire with powerful water jets to prevent its spread. Even though this was an outdoor fire, BA was required in the down-wind smoke plume. The front cover of this book shows another dramatic view of this particular fire.*

**2001    Crawshaw High School, Pudsey, Leeds**

*Over 1,000 school children were displaced when yet another major school fire occurred. This broke out early in the evening, and this time was believed to be caused by an electrical fault. Firefighters successfully fought to cut the fire off at one end of the complex, but despite this considerable damage and disruption to the school's activities was caused.*

**2002    Rescue From Sewer Shaft Workings, Stourton, Leeds (Right)**

*When a contractor fell down a 12-metre shaft at the site of new sewer workings, West Yorkshire firefighters were called to extricate him from his plight. After descending to the casualty in the very confined space, rescue crews carefully placed him in a specialist stretcher whilst colleagues above rigged lines before the worker was safely hauled up to street level and taken to hospital.*

**2002     Osborne Road, Birkby, Huddersfield (Left)**

*This incident was one of the worst fatal fires attended by West Yorkshire crews in recent years. Following an arson attack on the terraced house, eight members of one family lost their lives. After a forensic examination by West Yorkshire fire officers and police at the scene, three men were charged with murder, found guilty and jailed.*

**2003     Rawson's Mill, Barnsley Road, Portobello, Wakefield**

*Shortly after the day's production started at a textile manufacturers, a fire broke out in a production machine. As all 250 employees safely evacuated the premises, firefighters used fifteen pumps to tackle the fire on the site which is bordered by the River Calder. The use of a firefighter's historic main weapon – water – is very well illustrated in this maze of hoses.*

2003     Styrene Packaging, Park House Road, Low Moor, Bradford (Left)

*This twenty pump fire involving 100 firefighters created vast volumes of toxic smoke before it came under control. In addition to the pumping appliances, an aerial ladder platform (ALP) and a turntable ladder (TL) were deployed at strategic points to provide powerful firefighting jets above the fire. This view shows the ALP at work in the foreground with its firefighter operator manning the controls and keeping a careful watch on the crew working in the cage above. The TL can also be seen at work on the left of the image.*

2003     Cotewall Road, West Bowling, Bradford

*A dramatic image of a West Yorkshire Fire & Rescue Service crew rigged in breathing apparatus getting close to deep-seated fire in an unofficial dump of 5,000 old tyres. Due to the poisonous smoke cloud motorists were diverted from the scene and the residents of neighbouring properties were advised to keep their windows closed during this protracted incident.*

**2004     Victoria Park Special School, Bramley, Leeds**

*West Yorkshire fire crews were called to this school late one evening to find a serious fire. At its height 100 firefighters tackled the flames. The operation to save the building was hampered by a lack of water pressure on the site and strong, blustery winds. Subsequent forensic investigations indicated that the fire had been deliberately lit.*

**2005     Decosol, Shelf, Halifax**

*This fire involved a converted mill being used as a warehouse storing hundreds of thousands of alcohol and oil-based car products in bottles and aerosol cans. Adjacent to the building were six 10,000-litre ethanol tanks. The fire at one end of the building was already well advanced when the first crews arrived and not long afterwards a sudden explosive ignition, known to firefighters as a flashover, blew out the gable end wall of the old mill. Fortunately no crews were in the immediate vicinity when this happened, but the close proximity of a fuel station created an additional risk before the fire was brought under control.*

**2005     Northbound A1, Wentbridge**

*When an articulated HGV lorry carrying steel girders crashed though the south-bound carriageway of the A1, it collided with a van and several other vehicles travelling in the north-bound lane and several drivers were trapped in the wreckage. The rescue operation, in conjunction with medical and paramedic crews, was a complicated and lengthy one and these views show the extrication of casualties in progress, using a range of hydraulic tools and air lifting bags. Sadly, one driver was killed and several others seriously injured.*

**2007    Hay & Company, Brick Lane Mills, Thornton Road, Bradford**

*Two neighbouring streets were evacuated when firefighters were called to a fire in a disused mill and the residents were temporarily housed at a nearby sports centre. The fire rapidly developed to involve the whole of the mill structure and this view shows some of the 100 firefighters deployed at the scene as they ran out additional lines of hose in order to restrict the spread of fire to nearby houses.*

**2009     Carleton High School, Pontefract**

*In this image, West Yorkshire firefighters are concentrating their powerful water jets to prevent the main body of the fire in the background from spreading to the section of the school buildings on the left of the photograph. Many UK school buildings built in the last few decades have been of light construction, allowing fire to spread very rapidly. By 2009 the direct cost of school fires was running to over £70 million per year. Thanks to a long campaign led by the then-Chief Fire Officer of West Yorkshire in 2007, the Government's expectation was that in the majority of cases, the installation of sprinkler systems in schools would take place.*

**2010     Natasha's School Uniform Shop, Westgate, Bradford**

*This outbreak of fire in a Bradford city centre shop was quickly attacked by breathing apparatus crews. Fifty firefighters successfully extinguished the flames and prevented a spread to adjacent shop premises.*

**2010    Line Rescue Training, Galpharm Stadium, Huddersfield**

*For all specialist fire service teams, regular realistic training is essential to maintain their skills and competences. Here, members of West Yorkshire's line rescue team are practising their line lowering techniques using the various structures of the Galpharm Stadium.*

**2011    Water Rescue Exercise, Castleford (Right)**

*Water rescue is another developing area of operational work for the fire service and, for West Yorkshire crews, this is no exception. Here, in conjunction with a paramedic crew, a simulated casualty has been pulled from the river, placed upon a special stretcher and pulled up to safety.*

**2011    Gas Explosion, Rhodes Street, Hightown, Castleford**

*Firefighters were called at 0130 hours to what they believed was a small kitchen fire only to find a string of small fires in a row of six terraced houses. The crews swiftly evacuated the residents and shortly afterwards an explosion blew off the roofs of some of the properties, showering debris into a wide area across the street. It is believed that the theft of copper cabling from an empty property earlier in the evening may have contributed to a gas leak, the fires and the explosion. Thanks to the rapid intervention of the firefighters, there were no injuries to residents, although one firefighter suffered minor cuts and bruises.*

# Suspect trapped in well

A BURGLARY suspect was trapped in a well for three hours yesterday – after falling in while being chased by neighbours of his alleged victim.

The 21-year-old man dialled 999 from his mobile phone just after 5am yesterday to complain he was trapped at the bottom of the 30ft deep well in Halifax.

He was rescued by firefighters just before 8am and taken to hospital suffering from a fractured vertebrae in his back.

The man fell down the well, with a 5ft diameter, after vaulting a wall at St Thomas' Church in Claremount Road, Boothtown.

Police had earlier been called to a house in nearby Bell Street, Boothtown, to reports of a burglary.

The man was arrested on suspicion of burglary before being taken to Huddersfield Royal Infirmary for treatment.

**2011    Line Rescue, Claremont Road, Boothtown, Halifax**

*This view shows the West Yorkshire Fire & Rescue Service line rescue team, together with paramedics, effecting the actual rescue of a burglar from a steep hillside above an industrial site. Here, he is being fitted in a special sling prior to being lowered safely to ground level. Article © Halifax Courier.*

**2012    Urban Search and Rescue Exercise, Huddersfield**

*Similar to line rescue, the fire service in recent decades has developed Urban Search and Rescue (USAR), which embodies techniques and specialist equipment for locating and extricating persons trapped beneath debris in collapsed buildings or from other confined space entrapment. This exercise simulated the rescue of a building worker trapped in underground workings.*

**2012    Urban Search and Rescue Dog, Dewsbury**

*West Yorkshire Fire & Rescue Service has several dogs on its operational team for working with USAR teams during the location of buried casualties and for assisting forensic investigation into the cause of a fire where suspicious circumstances might suggest arson. Here, during an exercise, Firefighter Darren Booth, the dog's handler, works with Spencer at the scene of a USAR exercise.*

**2012     Training Centre, Birkenshaw**

*Not for the faint-hearted! During 2013, the BBC TV show* The One Show *visited West Yorkshire Fire & Rescue Service Headquarters. Here, in the last weeks prior to his retirement, Photographic Manager Brian Saville (middle) accompanies BBC presenter Jamie Crawford (right) and a West Yorkshire training instructor in a Fire Behaviour Training Unit in which firefighters practise their techniques under very realistic and hot conditions.*

**2012     Training Centre, Birkenshaw**

*During the BBC's filming session, four Fire Behaviour Training instructors show their working rig to the camera against a rather warm background.*

**2013     Ripponden Moor, Rochdale Road, Ripponden**

*The growing incidence of very dry summers has created a challenge to fire services in dealing with difficult and protracted heath and grassland fires. Such fires in hot weather are physically demanding for the crews concerned, and require special skills to maximise the available water supplies for firefighting over very widespread rural areas, as can be seen from these two images of a typical West Yorkshire incident.*

2013    Horse Rescue, Gibb Lane, Mount Tabor, Halifax

*Firefighters came to the rescue of this horse which had fallen through the ice on a frozen lake in a quarry during a bitterly cold winter's night. Here, a member of the crew comforts the rescued animal whilst awaiting specialist veterinary assistance.*

**2013     Water Rescue, Tees Barrage**

*A realistic training session in some fast water as the 'rescuer' moves to safely secure the 'casualty'.*

**2014     West Yorkshire Fire & Rescue Service Visual Aids Department**

*The camera captures the unique West Yorkshire Fire & Rescue Service Visual Aids Department photographic trio who, collectively over four decades, have provided the majority of the dramatic images which appear throughout the pages of this book.*
*From left to right:  Andrew Hanson, Brian Saville and Ken Wilkinson.*

# APPENDICES 103

APPENDIX I

WEST YORKSHIRE FIRE & RESCUE SERVICE – THE ORGANISATION

WEST YORKSHIRE FIRE & Rescue Service provides a professional and skilled emergency response service twenty-four hours per day, every day of the year, as well as providing a range of other services and functions.

This is how the Brigade projects its aims and objectives in its public leaflets and information:

## Prevention

We believe the most effective way to save lives, reduce injuries and other losses is to reduce the number of incidents which occur. We do this by focusing on risk reduction for vulnerable people and by raising awareness about risk to the wider community and how people can prevent fires and other emergencies occurring through safer behaviour and practice both at home and at work.

## Education

We engage with communities and agencies to identify and reduce risks from fire and other hazards. We visit schools and community groups to deliver educational programmes. We also provide programmes to young people, such as the highly successful Young Firefighters Scheme and Safety Rangers. We also have in place risk reduction teams to access and engage with those people most vulnerable to fire and provide information, education and supply protection measures.

We have a learning resource centre originally called Safety Central, based in the old Bramley Fire Station, Leeds, but now renamed Service Delivery Centre which is the centre of excellence for the development and delivery of fire and safety education and awareness.

## Protecting

We have a dedicated enforcement team who provide advice, guidance and support to workplaces and other buildings to help them comply with legal standards of fire safety in discharging our statutory duties. We carry out operational fire risk assessments on non-domestic properties and we have Arson Task Forces, which work towards reducing the deliberate and nuisance fires in West Yorkshire.

## Responding

*We fight fires* – Our Mobilising and Communications Centre, or Brigade Control, as it is known, takes emergency 999 calls and dispatches our front-line appliances. All appliances boast state-of-the-art equipment. We also have a number of specialist appliances to deal with a range of different incidents, such as flooding, rescue from height etc. We also have appliances provided by government to deal with national incidents.

On arrival, our firefighters are trained to use their expertise to extinguish the fire and minimise damage to property. Following a fire we will provide advice to those in the immediate location in an attempt to highlight and thus prevent further incidence.

*We rescue people* – Skilled firefighters using the latest equipment and techniques will respond to all incidents where people become trapped. Examples of these are road traffic collisions, building collapse and lift rescue. Our firefighters are highly trained in first aid and trauma care.

*We rescue animals* – By working closely with the RSPCA if an animal is in distress we can, if necessary, assist with the safe rescue of both small and large animals.

*We deal with other emergencies* – We are trained and equipped to deal with a wide variety of everyday and headline hitting emergencies such as spillages of dangerous chemicals, local and wide area flooding, road traffic collisions, aircraft and railway incidents.

Our ambition is: Making West Yorkshire Safer.

Our aim is to provide an excellent Fire and Rescue Service working in partnership to reduce death, injury and economic loss and contribute to community well-being.

APPENDIX 2

HANDLING WEST YORKSHIRE'S 999 FIRE AND RESCUE CALLS:
A BRIEF HISTORY OF BRIGADE CONTROL

THE BRIGADE'S 999 call handling Centre has a complicated history.

Prior to 1972, Brigade Control was located in the current Centre's underground basement and was responsible for the West Riding Fire Brigade. The City Brigades (known then as County Borough Brigades) – Huddersfield, Dewsbury, Bradford, Leeds and Wakefield had smaller, independent Control rooms. Following extensive alterations, Brigade Control was relocated above ground at the present location, but remained under the control of the WRCC.

The West Yorkshire Fire Service was formed in 1974 when the West Riding and County Borough Brigades were amalgamated into the one enlarged Brigade. The smaller City Control rooms were closed and the staff relocated to Fire Service Headquarters at Birkenshaw where this central Control room received all fire and other emergency calls for the fire service across West Yorkshire. In those days, the mobilising staff used simple card wheel indexes to assist with address locations, formulate attendances and mobilise the appropriate fire stations. This manual system at Brigade Control continued in use until April 1987.

*The Brigade's 999 Call Centre, 1987*

Following a major investment in the building, a new extension was built to house the Control room with air conditioning and secure power supplies and the Brigade's first computerised mobilising system (IAL's Firewatch) was procured. This system was able to track all the Brigade's fire engines and resources and automatically provided the mobilising staff with suggested pre-determined attendances. An advanced communications package was also introduced.

June 1999 saw Brigade Control returning to the Headquarters basement as a temporary measure to allow for further comprehensive building work and the upgrading of the computer systems to utilise Motorola's Pro Cad software for dealing with 999 calls and mobilizing. This upgrade also included a new mapping feature to assist with the precise location of emergency incidents.

Brigade Control resurfaced in 2000 into its new state of the art building with its innovative communication and mobilising systems. During 2009 the Brigade's radio scheme was upgraded to the national digital radio system called Firelink and in the summer of 2011, the latest software was introduced into the 999 mobilising system.

Due to the government's termination of the 'FireControl' project in December 2010, a comprehensive review was held into the core functions, systems and methods of working of Brigade Control, in order to maintain its effective role in the future as the Brigade's mobilising and communications centre.

As a result, a new Fire Control Centre will be introduced in the spring of 2014, located in Leeds.

APPENDIX 3
FIRE SAFETY IN WEST YORKSHIRE

Up until recently, fire precautions have been driven by 'stable door' legislation due to various fire disasters that have happened over the last 200 years. More recently, the fires at Eastwood Mills, Keighley, in February 1956 in which eight people died; the Top Storey Club, Bolton, in May 1961 where nineteen people perished; and at William Henderson and Sons department store, Liverpool, in June 1960 where ten people were trapped on the third floor even though the brigade arrived within two minutes of being called, resulted in fire brigades being given the power to inspect factories for fire safety.

There were also further amendments to the fire sections contained in the Factories Act 1961, the Licensing Act 1961 and the Offices, Shops and Railway Premises Act 1963 which led to the production of fire certificates to include not only means of escape, but also provision for fighting fire and structural fire separation.

*Chief Fire Officer Graham Karran QFSM FIFireE CFO, 1983–1990.*

The main trigger, however, for full Fire Authority involvement came with the fire at the Rose and Crown Hotel, Saffron Walden, on Boxing Day 1969. Despite the efforts of fire crews, eleven residents died in the smoke although seventeen were rescued. This particular fire prompted the Government to look at the whole structure of fire safety legislation, and as a result, in 1971 the Fire Precautions Act passed into law.

Following the fateful fire on 11 May 1985 at the Bradford City football ground, West Yorkshire, where fifty-six people died and many were seriously injured, recommendations again led to the Fire Safety and Safety of Places of Sport Act 1987. European directives also led to changes in legislation again in 1997 with the Fire Precautions (Workplace) Regulation being enacted.

For over thirty years, regulation had made fire safety matters prescriptive but increasingly out-dated and unnecessarily bureaucratic, so that in 2005 the Regulatory Reform (Fire Safety) Order came into effect to replace over seventy separate pieces of fire safety law. The new Order applied fire safety to all places that are non-domestic premises, with a general duty to ensure, so far as is reasonably practicable, the safety of employees and other persons, together with a duty to carry out a fire risk assessment.

As the number of lives thankfully lost in fires in commercial premises have progressively become few and far between, partly due to fire safety work of fire brigades, the concept of prevention in domestic property gained speed in the late 1970s as up to 800 people a year were dying in house fires. Cheaper more effective smoke detectors and the dedication of the fire service and its staff over the last thirty-five years has contributed to a significant achievement in the reduction of lives lost in house fires.

Over the last ten years, West Yorkshire has adopted a very pro-active approach to delivering the fire safety message, with an education programme in conjunction with local schools. In addition, some 60,000 home fire safety checks have been delivered each year, including the fitting of smoke alarms, and all manner of supporting initiatives have been developed, such as the chip pan display vehicle which can graphically show with real flames the dangers of a chip pan fire in the home.

The core ambition is to make West Yorkshire safer by reducing deaths, injuries, economic loss from fire, and contribute to community well-being. In 2009, the Brigade's pioneering safety education centre called Safety Central was opened on the site of the old Bramley Fire Station. It is staffed by the Brigade's highly motivated Prevention and Protection personnel who undertake a wide range of safety duties and involvement with the communities of West Yorkshire. Safety Central was renamed the Service Delivery Centre in 2014.

*Chief Fire Officer Phil Toase CBE QFSM BSc MCGI FIFireE CFO, 2000–2008.*

## APPENDIX 4
### VICTORY FOR SCHOOL SPRINKLER CAMPAIGN

In 2007, an eight-year campaign for the installation of fire sprinklers in all new and refurbished school buildings was finally won. West Yorkshire's then-Chief Fire Officer, Phil Toase, was able to give his crusade renewed impetus through his Presidency of the influential Chief Fire Officers' Association (CFOA).

Property losses from UK school fires, many of which are started deliberately, run to more than £70 million a year. Fortunately, no child has been killed but there have been several incidents where death or injury were only narrowly avoided. In 2006, CFOA warned Schools Minister Jim Knight that it was only a question of time before tragedy struck. Their call for immediate action was backed in an unprecedented move by every CFO in the country.

Mr Knight said that new schools, or those undergoing major refurbishment using public funds, would have to complete a risk analysis to decide whether they should be fitted with sprinklers. In effect, the Government's expectation was that in the majority of cases this will lead to the installation of sprinklers.

'Over the past eight years there has been mounting pressure from CFOA, the Local Government Association, the Fire Brigades Union, the National Union of Teachers and hundreds of individual Members of Parliament on this issue,' explained Mr Toase. West Yorkshire Fire Authority elected members, who had also championed sprinklers at the highest political level, said they had been proud to be in the vanguard of the sprinkler campaign and had reached agreement with all five local education authorities to fit sprinklers in new schools across West Yorkshire.

The Authority Chair said it had also worked closely with housing groups to promote and target the fitting of sprinklers in residential and domestic premises where the occupants were identified to be at highest risk. Success in this area has included the fitting of sprinklers in residential care homes, sheltered housing complexes, houses in multiple occupation, fire stations and private homes.


APPENDIX 5

WEST YORKSHIRE FIRE & RESCUE SERVICE TRAINING CENTRE

The current West Yorkshire Fire Service Multi-Purpose Training Centre at Headquarters at Birkenshaw was opened in 1991.

This new development replaced the old smoke house which was demolished a few years ago and the new Technical Rescue Training Centre building was built on that site. The MPTC is used as a multi-purpose heat and smoke training facility, mainly breathing apparatus (BA) related. The building offers real fire training on one side (hot side) and guideline search & rescue on the other (cold side). The building is also used for ladder training, confined space rescues and other command and control exercises.

The main Training Centre building has three floors. The first and second are recruit dormitories and the third floor is used by Fire Safety. There are five classrooms, although the majority of theoretical recruit training is undertaken in the Demonstration Room.

The Training Centre currently delivers courses which include all aspects of Recruit Training, Operational Driver Training, Breathing Apparatus, Road Traffic Collision, Rope Rescue, Water Rescue, Hazardous Materials, First Aid / Casualty Care responders, Command

*Chief Fire Officer James Manuel QFSM FIFireE CFO, 1989–1999.*

and Control simulations and exercises and Operational Commander Development.

Some international students have been trained at Birkenshaw, as from time to time have a number of recruits from other UK fire and rescue services.


APPENDIX 6

WEST YORKSHIRE FIRE APPLIANCES: A BRIEF OVERVIEW FROM 1974 TO DATE

The formation of the West Yorkshire Fire Service in 1975 combined a mixed fleet of fire appliances from across the districts. This meant inheriting the ex-county borough and city fire brigade appliances and specialist vehicles, consisting of such diverse makes as Dennis, AEC, Albion, Ford, Bedford and Dodge. These were supplied as water tenders and specials to JCDD Home Office specification. The aerial appliances were made up of 70ft Simon snorkel, 50ft Simon platforms, one 70ft Orbitor, 50ft Simonitors and 100ft Merryweather A and B type turntable ladders.

The first appliances ordered by the new West Yorkshire authority in 1976 were supplied by Cheshire Fire Engineering of Sandbach. This company was an old established coach-building firm which had been known as Jennings Coachworks. This contract supplied long and short wheelbase pumping appliances with the first of the Godiva multi-pressure fire pumps with a capacity of supplying 1,000 gallons per minute.

The next contract in 1978 then converted to the Dennis series appliances, supplied by the original Dennis factory in Guildford. This contract applied to the new Dennis RS series and subsequently changed to the Dennis SS series. These appliances were in the first generation to embody Alison Automatic transmissions. The policy on special appliances at this time was to re-chassis the aged Merryweather turntable ladders being mounted on the new Dennis F128, or Delta chassis.

The next contract in 1982 then converted to the Shelvoke & Drewery appliance as Dennis Fire had gone into liquidation. The Shelvoke & Drewery appliance had the first all-tilt drivers and crew cab, which was a chassis converted from the municipal market. In 1984, local manufacturer Angloco of Batley supplied a series of appliances on the Bedford TK chassis with automatic transmission.

1986 saw Saxon of Cheshire supply a series of appliances with the Dodge G13 Commando highline cab with automatic transmission. In the same year a Chemical Cleansing Unit was supplied by Angloco of Batley on a Bedford TL Chassis. Two new aerial 100ft Magirus turntable ladders were also supplied by Carmichaels of West Bromwich.

Bedford then entered the West Yorkshire fleet once again in 1986 with a series of new type Bedford TL appliances being supplied by HCB Angus of Southampton. These appliances were supplied with a manual gearbox, and the Godiva UMPX 750 gallon per minute pump. In 1988 a Metz 100ft turntable ladder was supplied by Angloco of Batley.

The next contract saw the introduction of the first Swedish Volvo appliance as Bedford, Dodge, and Shelvoke & Drewry followed the path of Dennis into liquidation. The Volvo FL Range had to undergo enhancements to meet the stringent JCCD Home Office specifications. The first Volvo appliance of 1987 was stationed at Bingley Fire Station. HCB Angus of Southampton supplied the Volvo appliances for eight years until 1994.

In 1995 Emergency One of New Cumnock, Scotland, was awarded the contract to supply Volvo appliances and subsequently won the contract up until 2009, in total supplying more than 100 Volvo appliances to West Yorkshire. The 100th appliance was a Volvo pump for Todmorden Fire Station with the registration number R822 CUA.

2009 saw the contract for appliances going to the Firebuy national contract and awarded to John Dennis of Guildford for the supply of eighteen heavy rescue tenders, whilst in the same year, Emergency One was awarded the contract for two MAN heavy rescue tenders, both with automatic transmission and 4 x 4 drive. The new copolymer plastic bodywork was now introduced as standard on the West Yorkshire Fire and Rescue Appliance User Requirement specification. Both contracts supplied the new bodywork material, with the advantage of this material being the option of a re-useable 'second life' bodywork.

In 2009 two combined aerial rescue pumps were also commissioned, on Volvo FM9, 18-tonne, 2-axle chassis. The aerial capability was the Magirus Multistar 30-metre aluminium boom with rescue cage and Alufire superstructure bodywork, whilst the fire pump was the Godiva Prima triple stage, with the ability to deliver 4000litres/min at 10 bar and 1000-litre water tank.

During the same year WH Bence of Bristol supplied a command unit on a Volvo FLL 15-tonne chassis with manual transmission. This new unit possessed new and enhanced command and control facilities with a roof mounted satellite receiver. WH Bence also supplied two first of type welfare units on converted 3.5-tonne Citroen relay vans. Water rescue capability was introduced with the supply of two 4 x 4 converted Ford Transit vans with inflatable dinghies and two Toyota Hilux 4 x 4 utility vehicles to tow boat trailers with hard ribbed inflatable dinghies. Six young firefighters' (cadet) vehicles were supplied by Angloco of Batley and funded by sponsorship from local businesses in the West Yorkshire area. These vehicles were converted Citroen Relay 3.5 tonne vans, with crew compartments and Rosenbauer Otter fire pump with manual primer.

Then, in 2011 WH Bence supplied a technical rescue vehicle (TRV) on a Volvo FM9 chassis with powertronic automatic gearbox, 18 tonne GVW which also incorporated copolymer plastic bodywork.

In 2012 a three-year contract for heavy rescue pumping appliances was awarded to Emergency One UK as part of the consortium framework agreement. In the first year five Volvo heavy rescue pumping appliances were to be delivered, with a further six the following year.

Two more combined aerial rescue pumps with improved specification and a higher gross vehicle weight capacity of 23.5 tonnes and third axle configuration and an improved 1500-litre water tank capacity were added to the fleet.

## APPENDIX 7
SOME FACTS ABOUT THE UNIFORM WORN BY WEST YORKSHIRE'S FIREFIGHTERS

### 1980s

At this time, cork fire helmets were used by firefighters and had no visor. Yellow plastic over-trousers were also worn, as well as plastic handling gloves, rubber boots and Melton wool fire tunics. This uniform had remained largely unchanged since the Second World War and was worn by most British firefighters.

### 1985

The first 'modern' fire kit was developed, known as a 'layered' construction. For the first time these layers were both made of the same material. The outer material consisted of 'Nomex', which is fire resistant and the tunic and trousers had a waterproof liner and a thermal inner material.

### 1987

Plastic fire gloves gave way to leather.

### Circa 1990

A change from traditional cork fire helmets to the new-style Cromwell F500 helmet. This was the first new-generation helmet to have a plastic visor.

### 1998

The 'managed personal protective equipment (PPE) system' was introduced into West Yorkshire Fire Service. Prior to 1998, there had been problems with fire kit being repaired and returned on time. Previously, everyone had two or three fire kits issued to them. The 'managed system' was unique to the Brigade and meant every firefighter was issued with one set of kit and each station had a stock of spares. It removed individual ownership and meant that personnel would get replacement kit instantly, rather than having to wait months for repairs. It was a vastly improved system and many other brigades followed suit.

## 1999

A change of helmet to Cromwell F600, which was a more encompassing 'jet style' design. This year also saw the introduction of the current type of fire hood, which is made of P84 fireproof Lenzing material.

## 2002

The introduction of leather fire boots. Each operational firefighter was issued with one pair of leather and one pair of rubber. Prior to then, they were issued with just one pair of rubber boots.

## 2009

A change to the current Rosenbauer fire helmet, which meets all the latest EU specification regarding safety and performance.

## 2012–2013

It is intended that West Yorkshire firefighters, fire kit will be upgraded yet again as standards and protection levels are continually improved. On 30th March 2012 the Authority's Executive Committee approved a report seeking to replace the current PPE of tunics and over-trousers with garments manufactured by Bristol Uniforms. This saw tunics and over-trousers with a gold PBI outer fabric and a Gore-Tex cross tech fire blocker membrane and quilted Nomex viscose lining. The new firefighters' PPE was put into service in January 2013.


APPENDIX 8

THREE NEW WEST YORKSHIRE FIRE STATIONS

Two new West Yorkshire fire stations in Pontefract and Normanton were officially opened by the Lord Lieutenant of West Yorkshire, Dr Ingrid Roscoe on 27th April 2012. Pontefract became the first 'Blue Light' complex in the county, with West Yorkshire Police and Yorkshire Ambulance Service sharing the facilities.

The Pontefract station, on Stump Cross Lane, enjoys excellent access to key road networks and is mid-way between the former Pontefract and Knottingley stations, which it replaces.

The £2 million Pontefract/Knottingley merger was first proposed back in 2006 to underpin a major revamp of fire and rescue cover across the Five Towns but the project as a whole was frustrated by land purchase problems and other technical issues. Work finally began in March 2010.

The Pontefract building was constructed by ISG Construction plc and the station houses two fire engines, a gym, recreational area and meeting rooms as well as incorporating the latest high performance materials, rainwater harvesting and solar panels. It also hosts a steel-framed training tower for rescue exercises.

At the opening Chief Fire Officer Simon Pilling welcomed local collaboration with police and ambulance services. 'Improved co-operation across the 'Blue Lights' will lead to more effective working and help all three agencies maintain cost-effective, resilient services to the public and local businesses alike,' he added.

Councillor David Ridgway, who chaired West Yorkshire Fire and Rescue Authority at the time, said that the Brigade prided itself on innovation and forward-thinking ideas like the sharing of facilities at Pontefract and the new crewing system at Normanton were excellent examples of how more could be delivered with less.

Chief Superintendent Marc Callaghan, Wakefield District Police Divisional Commander, said: 'The move to Pontefract Fire Station is an excellent opportunity ensuring that the Pontefract and Knottingley NPT remains at the heart of the communities it serves.'

Paul Mudd, Locality Director for Emergency Operations (West Yorkshire) at Yorkshire Ambulance Service NHS Trust, said: 'Our priority is to respond to 999 calls as quickly as possible and by having ambulances strategically located, where historically there has been a high level of demand, we are reaching patients quicker than ever before. The fire station at Pontefract will become part of our network of these locations across West Yorkshire and we are delighted to be working alongside our emergency service partners for the benefit of patients in the area.'

Normanton Fire Station was completed by Caddick Construction plc, and was been built on the site of the old station at The Grove and on adjoining land at Princess Street which now provides the main entrance.

A nearby house has also been converted to provide accommodation for five firefighters operating the day-crewing/close call system. The new building is larger than the old one and provides two appliance bays, a gym, workshop, offices and meetings rooms. It also boasts a training tower and environmentally-friendly features including rainwater harvesting and solar panels to pre-heat the domestic hot water supply.

The redevelopment cost £1.7m. Discussions are on-going regarding inter-agency collaboration at Normanton. Chief Fire Officer Pilling said both projects helped to secure fire cover for the area.

A full refurbishment of Castleford Fire Station was also achieved in 2012/13 to provide co-location accommodation for fire and police teams. A purpose built residential block was also included in the construction scheme to allow for revision of staffing arrangements from the previous shift system to the innovative day crewing close call model.

West Yorkshire Fire and Rescue Authority have also successfully procured new land sites at Rastrick, South Kirby, Dewsbury and Killingbeck in Leeds as part of its ambitious programme to reshape emergency response provision across the county with the construction of new fire stations. Further land sites are being assessed in Bradford, North Leeds and Wakefield and will hopefully be procured during 2014.

APPENDIX 9
THE HISTORY OF OAKROYD HALL

## The Headquarters of West Yorkshire Fire & Rescue Service

The Ackroyd family purchased a cotton spinning and manufacturing business in a mill in Birkenshaw Bottom in 1832. Their other business interests included the Birkenshaw Saw Mills (now Farnells), and the Half Way House Colliery, so called because of its proximity to the Half Way House hostelry, an old coaching inn 'halfway' between Leeds and Halifax, and Bradford and Dewsbury, which still runs today, adjacent to the Headquarters site.

The family built Oakroyd Hall in 1867 on the site of the colliery and trees were planted to bind the earth and help prevent subsidence. At the main entrance to the grounds stood the lodge. This site is now occupied by semi-detached houses. From the Lodge ran a shale drive up to the front entrance of the Hall, the shale coming from the old mine workings.

In the area now used as the car park stood the stables, coach house and gardens. Greenhouses stood on the grounds now occupied by the Stores and Workshops. The boundary wall at the back of the Workshops had a very unusual feature. Incorporated in the wall were flues which were provided with heat from two boilers to enable grape-vines and tangerines to be grown against the wall.

Inside the Hall itself was a billiard room, which is today used as a conference room. In the wood panelling down the left-hand wall the remains of a door can be found leading to an underground room, which was used as a place of safety by one of the later occupiers. The Waiting Room was once a library and had a magnificent hand-carved wooden fireplace, but in later years this was removed and destroyed. A beautiful, fine marble fireplace was the feature of the Drawing Room (now the CAD Room) but this was also removed. Servants quarters and kitchens in the cellars and attics contrast starkly with the luxury the Ackroyd family must have enjoyed.

The West Riding County Council purchased the Hall in 1947 and it was used as a home for children who had been taken into care. In 1951 it passed into the hands of the War Department for use as an Administrative and Communications Centre. 1958 saw the premises again being sold back to the County Council and since 1964 it has been used for Fire Service purposes.

The Birkenshaw Parish Churchyard houses the 'Ackroyd Enclosure' which contains a mausoleum and family graves. The efforts of a Manpower Services team a few years ago cleared the site and much of interest was found there, but unfortunately nature has once again taken charge and it is again overgrown.

APPENDIX 10
IN THE LINE OF DUTY

Firefighting is a very dangerous profession and over the years firemen from the brigades that now make up West Yorkshire have lost their lives in the line of duty.

Although some of their names have long been forgotten they are remembered here:

Saved *by Charles Vigor reproduced by kind permission of the Fire Service College.*

Fireman John Hartley of the Leeds and Yorkshire Insurance Company,
6th January 1831

Superintendent William James of the Leeds Fire Brigade,
11th October 1857

Fireman Thomas Conway of the Bradford Fire Brigade,
23rd June 1889

Fireman Frank Clarke of the Bradford Fire Brigade,
23rd June 1889

Fireman James Potter Schofield of the London, Liverpool and Globe Insurance Company,
13th January 1892

Fireman James Harrison of the Greetland Fire Brigade,
21st December 1893

Fireman Joseph Ellis of the Leeds Fire Brigade,
30th March, 1897

Fireman Ebenezer Ineson of the Batley Fire Brigade,
14th April, 1900

Fireman Alexander Carmichael of the Brighouse Fire Brigade,
6th October 1903

Fireman  Herbert Storey of the Leeds Fire Brigade,
24th February 1909

Station Officer Charles Sugden of the Bradford Fire Brigade,
21st August 1916

Fireman Knighton Pridmore of the Bradford Fire Brigade,
21st August 1916

Fireman Fred Normington of the Bradford Fire Brigade,
21st August 1916

Fireman Eli Buckley of the Bradford Fire Brigade,
21st August 1916

Fireman Edgar Shaw of the Bradford Fire Brigade,
21st August 1916

Fireman Joseph Edmund Binns of the Bradford Fire Brigade,
21st August 1916

Fireman Fred Sharpe of the Dewsbury Fire Brigade,
22nd March 1919

Fireman Patrick Dunleavy of the Leeds Fire Brigade,
4th January 1922

Fireman Isaac Percival of the Leeds Fire Brigade,
18th January 1924

Fireman James Gavaghan of the Batley Fire Brigade,
17th July 1926

Fireman Henry Tindale of the Batley Fire Brigade,
17th July 1926

Fireman Alfred E. Waterhouse of the Leeds Fire Brigade,
31st December 1930

Section Leader Paul Cromwell of the National Fire Service (Leeds –
Park Street Station),
16th February 1944

Leading Fireman Walter Dutholt of the National Fire Service
(Farsley Station),
16th February 1944

Fireman Ernest Netherwood of the National Fire Service (Colne
Valley Station),
11th October 1947

Fireman Arnold Thomas Watson of the Halifax Fire Brigade,
27th June 1949

Fireman J. A. Thompson of the Wakefield City Fire Brigade,
14th June 1950

Chief Officer James H Pilling of the Leeds City Fire Brigade.
24th May 1954 (Grandfather of the current Chief Fire Officer,
S. Pilling)

Fireman Jack Wilkinson DCM of the Leeds City Fire Brigade,
1st October 1956

Fireman K. Gledhill of the West Riding County Fire Service,
25th May 1963

Fireman B. Ward of the West Riding County Fire Service,
14th May 1965

Fireman Hylton Brearley of the West Yorkshire Fire Service (Meltham),
14th December 1976

Fireman Jeffrey Naylor of the West Yorkshire Fire Service (Keighley),
10th July 1983

# FURTHER READING

Blackstone, G.V.,  *A History of the British Fire Service*, Routledge and Kegan Paul, 1957.

Firebrace, Sir Aylmer, *Fire Services Memories*,
Andrew Melrose, 1948.

Holloway, Sally, *Courage High*, HMSO, 1992.

Holloway, Sally and Wallington, Neil, *Fire and Rescue*, Patrick Stephens, 1994.

Honeycombe, Gordon, *Red Watch*, Hutchinson, 1976 and Jeremy Mills Publishing, 2007.

Ingham, H.S. (Editor), *Fire & Water – The London Firefighters' Blitz 1940–42 Remembered*, Firestorm Publications, 1992.

Morris, C.B., *Fire, Blackie and Son*, 1939.

Smith C.D, *The History of the Huddersfield Fire Brigade*, Kirklees Cultural Services, 1999.

Smith C.D, *The Leeds Fire Brigade*, Smith C.D, 2010

Wallington, Neil, *Firefighting – A Pictorial History*, Paragon, 1997.

Wallington, Neil, *In Case of Fire*, Jeremy Mills Publishing, 2005.

Wallington, Neil, *Out of the Flames, Fire Services National Benevolent Fund*, 2003.

Wallington, Neil, *One Hundred Years of the British Fire Engine*, Jeremy Mills Publishing, 2008.

# PHOTOGRAPHIC CAMERAS

Before the arrival of the digital camera age, the three West Yorkshire Fire & Rescue Service photographers carried Mamiya Medium Format 645 cameras.

Since the arrival of digital photographic technology to capture their graphic images both day and night the team have progressively utilised the Nikon D200; the D700 Digital; the D1X and the D3X – the latter model operates at twenty-four million pixels.

# ACKNOWLEDGEMENTS

The hard graft for any author is in the preparation of the subject matter of the book concerned. However, once Chief Fire Officer Simon Pilling had so readily blessed my early concept of this book, I was privileged to be granted not only full access to the Brigade's extensive photographic library to provide the core material of the book, but the welcome assistance of a small West Yorkshire team, drawn from both uniformed and support staff.

Consequently, my thanks must first go to Simon Pilling, who despite commanding a very large and busy Fire & Rescue Service, has always found time to give me his enthusiastic support for my project over the past two years and more. Then, of course, my sincere appreciation must go to the three West Yorkshire photographers themselves.

Firstly, to Brian Saville, who took those first early photographs for the Brigade's infant Visual Services Department almost four decades ago, and went on to win a number of national photographic awards, later to be joined by Andrew Hanson and Ken Wilkinson. Their quite fantastic visual images were often obtained under challenging physical situations close to firefighting operations. Such dramatic photographs as the trio have captured have made this book possible, and I trust it will stand as a collective graphic record of what the modern work of the British Fire and Rescue Service is all about.

My thanks are also due to other members of the small West Yorkshire team who aided my task, and a special mention is due to Chris Smith for his historical advice. Chris has published his own books on the former Leeds and Huddersfield Fire Brigades, so appreciated my task of selecting just over 100 images from the thousands in the Brigade's photographic library over its near forty-year history.

Then my further appreciation goes to Ray Banyard for his historical and photographic contribution, as well as that of Peter Buckland, Ben Bush, Kim Schofield, and Kelly Thornham. They all provided valuable information regarding the detail of many of the fires and other emergencies highlighted in this book. And to Angela Twigg, the Chief Officer's PA, go my thanks for so patiently acting as a gateway for my many enquiries during the period of preparing this work.

I must also applaud the vision of my publisher Jeremy Mills, together with the skills of his superb team of Hazel Goodes, Dawn Cockcroft, Paul Buckley and Abi Bliss in the design and production of Images of Fire.

Finally, once again I must pay tribute to the very significant assistance of my dear wife Susie. As with all my writing over past years, hers was a key part in bringing this book to fruition.

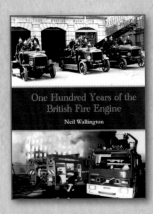

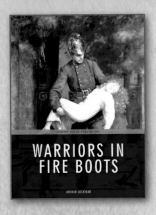
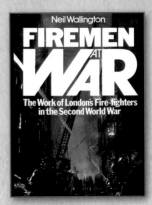

Published by Jeremy Mills Publishing Limited

113 Lidget Street
Lindley
Huddersfield
West Yorkshire HD3 3JR

www.jeremymillspublishing.co.uk

First published 2014

ISBN: 978-1-909837-15-7

Front cover image:
Fire at Pallet Yard, Horbury, Wakefield, 2001